Taylor Swift: From Country to Pop

Unofficial Biography

Lulu and Bell 2024

ISBN: 978-1-83990-407-3

Contents

Chapter 1: A Small Town Dreamer — 1-2

Chapter 2: Where It Started — 3-4

Chapter 3: Fearless — 5-6

Chapter 4: Speak Now: A Tale of Love and Independence — 7-8

Chapter 5: Red: Embracing Change and Vulnerability — 9-10

Chapter 6: 1989: Taylor Swift's Pop Revolution — 11-13

Chapter 7: Reputation: Taylor Swift's Bold Reinvention — 14-15

Chapter 8: Lover: Taylor Swift's Celebration of Love and Self-Discovery — 16-18

Chapter 9: Folklore and Evermore: Taylor Swift's Intimate Folk Chronicles — 19-20

Chapter 10: Sleepless Nights — 21-22

Quiz — 23-26

Conclusion — 27

Chapter 1: A Small Town Dreamer

Taylor Swift's story begins in Reading, Pennsylvania, where she was born on December 13, 1989, to Scott and Andrea Swift

PENNSYLVANIA SQUAD

Raised on a Christmas tree farm alongside her younger brother Austin, Taylor's childhood was filled with music and creativity. Her grandmother, an opera singer, ignited her passion for music, and Taylor began performing in local talent shows and events from a young age.

Despite her small-town upbringing, Taylor dreamed big. At just 12 years old, she started writing her own songs, pouring her heart and soul into every lyric. With a natural talent for storytelling and a knack for melodies, she quickly realized that music was her true calling. Taylor picked up the guitar and taught herself to play, spending hours perfecting her craft in her bedroom.

Fun fact about Taylor Swift's younger years is that she grew up on a farm and showed a deep passion for horseback riding. In fact, she competed in horse shows and even won several awards for her equestrian skills. This aspect of her life highlights her diverse interests and talents beyond music.

Chapter 2: Where It Started

At 14, Taylor convinced her parents to move to Nashville, Tennessee, the mecca of country music, to pursue her dreams of becoming a singer-songwriter.

Armed with determination and a notebook full of songs, she attended countless talent showcases and open mic nights, hoping to catch her big break.

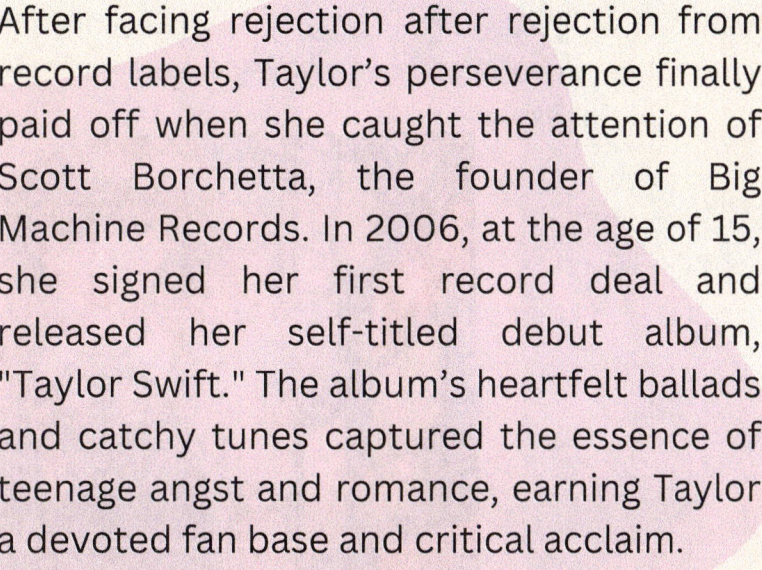

After facing rejection after rejection from record labels, Taylor's perseverance finally paid off when she caught the attention of Scott Borchetta, the founder of Big Machine Records. In 2006, at the age of 15, she signed her first record deal and released her self-titled debut album, "Taylor Swift." The album's heartfelt ballads and catchy tunes captured the essence of teenage angst and romance, earning Taylor a devoted fan base and critical acclaim.

Taylor Swift was the youngest songwriter ever hired by the Sony/ATV Tree publishing house. She signed with them at the age of just 14, demonstrating her exceptional talent and maturity as a songwriter even at such a young age. This early recognition and support from a prestigious publishing house played a significant role in launching her career in the music industry.

Chapter 3: Fearless

Taylor's sophomore album, "Fearless," marked a turning point in her career. Released in 2008, it showcased her growth as an artist and solidified her status as country music's brightest star.

With smash hits like "Love Story" and "You Belong with Me," Taylor dominated the charts and won over the hearts of teenagers worldwide with her relatable lyrics and infectious charm.

"Fearless" went on to become the best-selling album of 2009 and earned Taylor four Grammy Awards, including Album of the Year, making her the youngest artist ever to win the prestigious honor. At just 20 years old, Taylor had achieved more than most artists could dream of, but she was just getting started.

Taylor Swift not only achieved immense success with her music but also made a unique impact on the fashion world. She famously started the trend of wearing sundresses with cowboy boots, which became a signature look for her during that time. This fashion choice perfectly embodied the blend of country and pop influences in her music and helped solidify her image as a relatable yet stylish artist.

Chapter 4: Speak Now: A Tale of Love and Independence

Released in 2010, "Speak Now" marked a pivotal moment in Taylor Swift's career. Written entirely by Taylor herself, the album showcased her growth as a songwriter and storyteller.

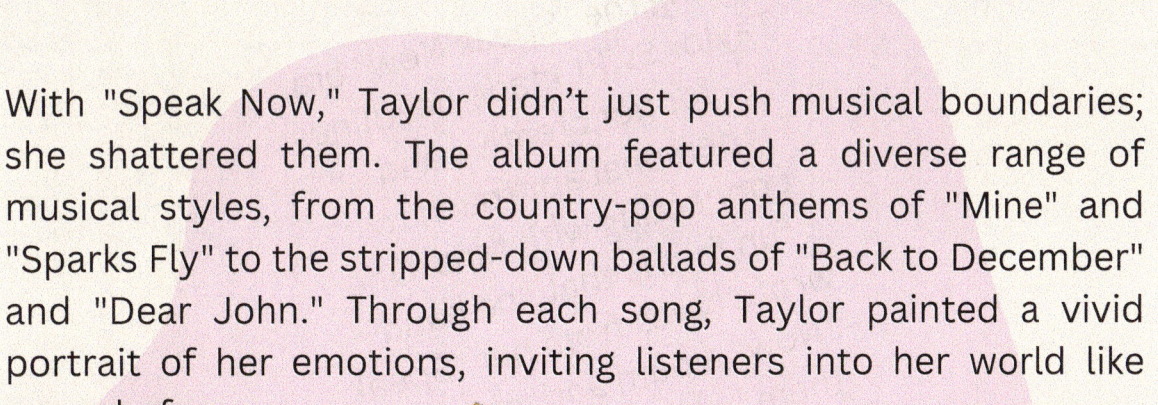

Each track was a glimpse into her heart and soul, chronicling her experiences with love, heartbreak, and self-discovery.

With "Speak Now," Taylor didn't just push musical boundaries; she shattered them. The album featured a diverse range of musical styles, from the country-pop anthems of "Mine" and "Sparks Fly" to the stripped-down ballads of "Back to December" and "Dear John." Through each song, Taylor painted a vivid portrait of her emotions, inviting listeners into her world like never before.

One of the standout tracks on "Speak Now" was "Mean," a defiant anthem against bullies and critics. With its infectious melody and empowering lyrics, the song resonated with fans of all ages, earning Taylor two Grammy Awards, including Best Country Song.

"Speak Now" was more than just an album; it was a declaration of independence and empowerment. Through her music, Taylor inspired fans to speak their truth, chase their dreams, and never apologize for who they are.

During the "Speak Now" era, Taylor Swift made headlines for her creative and personal approach to connecting with fans. One fun fact is that she hand-wrote lyrics from her "Speak Now" album and included them in the album's deluxe edition.

Chapter 5: Red: Embracing Change and Vulnerability

In 2012, Taylor Swift embarked on a new chapter in her career with the release of "Red." Inspired by the rollercoaster of emotions that comes with love and heartbreak, the album showcased a more mature and introspective side of Taylor's artistry.

"Red" was a departure from Taylor's previous work, incorporating elements of pop, rock, and even dubstep into her signature sound. Tracks like "I Knew You Were Trouble" and "22" were infectious pop anthems, while ballads like "All Too Well" and "Begin Again" showcased Taylor's vulnerability and depth as a songwriter.

One of the most iconic tracks on "Red" was "We Are Never Ever Getting Back Together," a catchy and relatable breakup anthem that topped charts around the world. With its infectious chorus and sassy lyrics, the song became an instant classic and further solidified Taylor's status as a pop powerhouse.

'CAUSE LOVING HIM WAS RED

"Red" received widespread critical acclaim and commercial success, earning Taylor numerous accolades and awards, including a Grammy nomination for Album of the Year. Through its diverse range of songs and emotions, "Red" captured the essence of Taylor's journey as an artist and a young woman navigating the complexities of love and life.

Chapter 6: 1989: Taylor Swift's Pop Revolution

In 2014, Taylor Swift embarked on a daring musical evolution with the release of her fifth studio album, "1989." Departing from her country roots, Taylor fully embraced a pop sound and image, marking a bold new chapter in her career.

Named after the year of her birth, "1989" was more than just an album; it was a love letter to the '80s, an era known for its infectious melodies and synth-driven pop anthems. With its sleek production, catchy hooks, and irresistible beats, "1989" captured the essence of a bygone era while still feeling fresh and modern.

The lead single, "Shake It Off," set the tone for the entire album with its upbeat tempo and empowering message of self-confidence and resilience. With its infectious chorus and playful lyrics, the song became an instant hit, topping charts around the world and earning Taylor widespread acclaim.

wildest dreams

But "1989" was more than just a collection of catchy pop tunes; it was a deeply personal and introspective album that showcased Taylor's growth as an artist and a young woman. Tracks like "Blank Space" and "Style" explored the complexities of love and relationships, while songs like "Wildest Dreams" and "Out of the Woods" delved into themes of nostalgia and self-discovery.

For the album 1989 Taylor Swift drew inspiration from '80s artists like Peter Gabriel and Annie Lennox

But "1989" was more than just a collection of catchy pop tunes; it was a deeply personal and introspective album that showcased Taylor's growth as an artist and a young woman. Tracks like "Blank Space" and "Style" explored the complexities of love and relationships, while songs like "Wildest Dreams" and "Out of the Woods" delved into themes of nostalgia and self-discovery.

"1989" was a critical and commercial juggernaut, earning Taylor numerous accolades and awards, including Album of the Year at the Grammy Awards. With its bold sound and infectious energy, the album solidified Taylor's status as a pop powerhouse and cemented her place in music history. Through "1989," Taylor proved that she was not afraid to take risks and push the boundaries of creativity, inspiring fans to embrace their authenticity and chase their dreams.

Chapter 7: Reputation: Taylor Swift's Bold Reinvention

In 2017, Taylor Swift emerged from the shadows with her sixth studio album, "Reputation," a bold and defiant statement that solidified her reputation as one of the most influential artists of her generation. Building on the themes of fame, love, and resilience, Taylor embraced a darker, edgier sound and image, reclaiming her narrative and proving that she was stronger than ever.

"Reputation" marked a departure from Taylor's previous work, both sonically and thematically. Fueled by the media scrutiny and personal struggles she faced in the public eye, the album delved into themes of betrayal, redemption, and self-discovery. With its sleek production, pulsating beats, and unapologetic lyrics, "Reputation" showcased a new side of Taylor's artistry while still staying true to her signature storytelling style.

The lead single, "Look What You Made Me Do," set the tone for the entire album with its dark and brooding vibe. With its biting lyrics and haunting melody, the song served as a defiant anthem against her detractors, signaling Taylor's readiness to reclaim her narrative and take back control of her reputation.

Delicate

But "Reputation" was more than just a collection of revenge anthems; it was a deeply personal and introspective album that explored the highs and lows of fame and relationships. Tracks like "Delicate" and "Getaway Car" showcased Taylor's vulnerability and depth as a songwriter, while songs like "End Game" and "This Is Why We Can't Have Nice Things" embraced a more playful and self-aware tone.

One of the standout tracks on "Reputation" was "New Year's Day," a tender ballad that served as a stark contrast to the album's darker themes. With its stripped-down production and heartfelt lyrics, the song served as a reminder of Taylor's roots as a storyteller and a romantic at heart.

Chapter 8: Lover: Taylor Swift's Celebration of Love and Self-Discovery

In 2019, Taylor Swift returned to the spotlight with her seventh studio album, "Lover," a radiant and joyous celebration of love, self-discovery, and empowerment. Departing from the darker themes of her previous album, "Reputation," Taylor embraced a more optimistic and romantic tone, inviting listeners into a world of love, nostalgia, and hope.

"Lover" marked a return to Taylor's roots as a storyteller and a romantic at heart. With its lush production, catchy melodies, and heartfelt lyrics, the album captured the essence of love in all its forms, from the exhilarating highs to the heartbreaking lows.

The lead single, "ME!," featuring Brendon Urie of Panic! At The Disco, set the tone for the entire album with its vibrant and whimsical vibe. With its upbeat tempo and empowering message of self-love and acceptance, the song became an instant hit, topping charts around the world and earning Taylor widespread acclaim.

Lover

But "Lover" was more than just a collection of love songs; it was a deeply personal and introspective album that explored Taylor's journey of self-discovery and growth. Tracks like "The Archer" and "Soon You'll Get Better" showcased Taylor's vulnerability and depth as a songwriter, while songs like "You Need to Calm Down" and "Miss Americana & The Heartbreak Prince" embraced a more playful and self-aware tone.

One of the standout tracks on "Lover" was the title track itself, a tender ballad that served as a love letter to Taylor's longtime partner, Joe Alwyn. With its heartfelt lyrics and dreamy melody, the song captured the essence of true love and commitment, inspiring listeners to cherish the ones they hold dear.

Lover is the first album she released under her new label, Republic Records, after parting ways with her longtime label, Big Machine Label Group.

Chapter 9: Folklore and Evermore: Taylor Swift's Intimate Folk Chronicles

In a surprising move in 2020, Taylor Swift treated fans to not just one, but two new albums: "Folklore" and "Evermore." Departing from her usual promotional cycle, Taylor dropped these albums with little warning, delighting fans with a double dose of her signature storytelling and introspective songwriting.

"Folklore," released in July 2020, marked a departure from Taylor's previous work both in its sound and thematic content. Produced in collaboration with Aaron Dessner of The National and Jack Antonoff, the album embraced a stripped-down, indie-folk sound, setting the stage for a collection of intimate and introspective tales.

"Folklore" was a departure from Taylor's usual autobiographical songwriting style, with many tracks exploring fictional characters and narratives. Songs like "The 1," "Exile" (featuring Bon Iver), and "Betty" captured the essence of human emotions and experiences with a raw and unfiltered honesty.

Following the success of "Folklore," Taylor surprised fans once again with the release of "Evermore" just five months later in December 2020. Billed as a sister album to "Folklore," "Evermore" continued the narrative threads and sonic landscape established in its predecessor.

Like "Folklore," "Evermore" explored themes of love, loss, and resilience, with Taylor once again delving into fictional characters and narratives. Tracks like "Gold Rush," "Tolerate It," and "Closure" offered glimpses into the lives of complex and multidimensional characters, each grappling with their own struggles and desires.

In summary, "Folklore" and "Evermore" represent a new chapter in Taylor Swift's career, showcasing her versatility as an artist and her ability to captivate listeners with her storytelling and songwriting prowess. With these albums, Taylor invites us into a world of imagination and introspection, reminding us of the power of music to transport us to new and unexpected places.

Chapter 10: Sleepless Nights

Midnights was released on October 21, 2022 and is Taylor Swift tenth studio album. Swift describes this album as "a collection of music written in the middle of the night, a journey through terrors and sweet dreams."

Midnights covered themes of heartbreak, love, self-reflection and revenge. The lead single of this album was Anti-hero which had a pop rock and 1980s inspired sound. The alum also includes tracks Lavender Haze and Karma.

meet me at midnight

Midnights moved away for the indie folk sound of Folklore and Evermore with its electronic and retro sound. Midnights was a huge success and broke multiple records on music streaming platforms and debuted in at least 14 countries at number one on their album charts.

Karma

Quiz

What is the title of Taylor Swift's debut single released in 2006?
a) "Tim McGraw"
b) "Teardrops on My Guitar"
c) "Our Song"
d) "Love Story"

What is the title of Taylor Swift's first live album, released in 2010?
a) Speak Now World Tour: Live
b) Fearless Tour: Live
c) Red Tour: Live
d) The 1989 World Tour: Live

Taylor Swift made her acting debut in which movie?
a) The Giver
b) Valentine's Day
c) Cats
d) The Hunger Games

Taylor Swift made her acting debut in which TV show?
a) Gossip Girl
b) Grey's Anatomy
c) Friends
d) CSI: Crime Scene Investigation

Which of the following awards has Taylor Swift NOT won?
a) Emmy Award
b) MTV Video Music Award
c) Academy of Country Music Award
d) Billboard Music Award

What is the title of Taylor Swift's documentary released in 2020?
a) Miss Americana
b) Reputation
c) 1989
d) Speak Now

Taylor Swift became the youngest recipient of the Grammy Award for Album of the Year. How old was she when she won it?
a) 18
b) 20
c) 22
d) 24

Taylor Swift famously wrote a song for a fellow artist. What is the name of the song she wrote for Little Big Town?
a) Better Man
b) Girl Crush
c) Pontoon
d) Day Drinking

Taylor Swift won the Grammy Award for Best Music Video for which song?
a) "Bad Blood"
b) "We Are Never Ever Getting Back Together"
c) "Delicate"
d) "Safe & Sound"

In 2020, Taylor Swift surprised fans by releasing an album with little prior announcement. What is the name of this album?
a) folklore
b) evermore
c) Lover
d) Red (Taylor's Version)

Which song did Taylor Swift perform at the 2019 Billboard Music Awards, marking her first televised performance of the song?
a) "ME!"
b) "You Need to Calm Down"
c) "The Archer"
d) "Lover"

What is the name of the character Taylor Swift voiced in the animated film "The Lorax"?
a) Audrey
b) Once-ler
c) Ted
d) Mayor O'Hare

Answers

1. a) "Tim McGraw"

2. a) Speak Now World Tour: Live

3. b) Valentine's Day

4. b) Grey's Anatomy

5. a) Emmy Award

6. a) Miss Americana

7. c) 22

8. a) Better Man

9. a) "Bad Blood"

10. a) folklore

11. d) "Lover"

12. a) Audrey

Conclusion

Taylor Swift's journey from a small-town dreamer to a global superstar is a testament to the power of perseverance, authenticity, and self-belief. Through her music and storytelling, she has inspired generations of teenagers to chase their dreams, embrace their flaws, and stand up for what they believe in. As Taylor continues to evolve as an artist and advocate, one thing remains constant: her unwavering commitment to being true to herself and her fans.

THIS IS OUR PLACE WE MAKE THE RULES

Printed by BoD™in Norderstedt, Germany